Unmasking Fear

A Life Strategies Experiential Handbook

∞

Jeanetta W. Dunlap, Ed. D.

Copyright © 2008 by Jeanetta W. Dunlap, Ed. D.

Library of Congress Control Number: 2008902530
ISBN: Softcover   978-1-4363-3010-7

All rights reserved. No part of this book may be reproduced or transmitted in any form or by any means, electronic or mechanical, including photocopying, recording, or by any information storage and retrieval system, without permission in writing from the copyright owner.

This book was printed in the United States of America.

To order additional copies of this book, contact:
Xlibris Corporation
1-888-795-4274
www.Xlibris.com
Orders@Xlibris.com

Contents

Acknowledgments 5

Foreword 6

Introduction 7

Spiritual Commentary On Fear 10

Thoughts Matter 14

Success-Itis Phobia 22

Things Are Not Always What They Seem 29

Suicide and Light Beyond Darkness 38

Entertaining Angels Unaware 47

God's Decision Making 53

Change 59

Stand . . . Stand . . . Stand 65

Conclusion 70

Glossary 71

Recommended Resources 73

Dedication

This book is lovingly dedicated in memory to my parents
Charles and Bertha

ACKNOWLEDGMENTS

A GENERAL ACKNOWLEDGMENT is given to all of the people who have inspired and assisted me on my spiritual journey. I am also grateful to Chief BJ (Betty Smith) for granting permission to cite selections from her inspirational meditation cards. About the cover photo: permission granted. The photograph depicts an early sunrise on Lake Ontario in upstate New York. Photographer credits are given posthumously to Doris M. Shaw.

FOREWORD

DURING THE YEARS, I have delivered lectures based on my personal experiences, and the events that have occurred in my life. I have revised and compiled shorter versions of some of these lectures into first person narrative essays.

The "First Person Narrative" essays are God-inspired. Biblical quotes are from the King James Bible. The narratives in this book were written with love and light. Like the sunflower, that always seeks the sun and grows towards the sun's light, I too, strive to stay in the God light by seeking and following the light of the (SON), Jesus the "I Am."

May you also, in your spiritual quest follow the lead of the sunflower, by turning your face to the sun, as a light seeker of the truth.

INTRODUCTION

WE TEND TO learn most often from our life experiences. We bring to these life experiences, our assumptions, and our beliefs, about the way we interact with self, other people, and situations in our environment. Experiential personal narrative essay vignettes included in this book, *Unmasking Fear*, are designed to identify with individual life experiences, and to help readers' learn to create positive thought patterns to release fear.

Developing positive thought patterns can be an effective life strategic tool to accomplish this task. Each person, experiences the world according to his, or her perspectives and learning styles. The structure of this book takes in consideration the different ways of individual learning – visual, auditory, and kinesthetic, through intuitive journaling exercises. One of the author's purposes is to provide a systematic handbook to help readers dispel myths about fear.

Another aim is to help readers find ways of clearing mental and emotional confusion through reflection. Reflective practices help in grasping insights that assist with self empowerment to overcome individual fears. To help in achieving this goal, the reader is provided with journaling, affirmations, and experiential activities. Journaling, affirmations, and experiential activities are aimed to help readers create a personal "Step by Step Development Plan" to overcome fear:

1. Identify the type of fear or fears. Consult Chief BJ's introductory meditation cards' contents to identify fear type.
2. Create a plan.
3. Implement the plan.

Each reader will need to develop an individual "Step by Step Development Plan" that fits his or her individual needs. The book will not provide the reader with a specific time frame for overcoming fears. Persistency and consistency are key factors, toward accomplishing the goal, of successfully, obtaining a relatively fear-free life style.

Persevere and Enjoy the Positive Change,

Jeanetta W. Dunlap, Ed.D.
February 2008

Spiritual Commentary On Fear

Picture yourself as a grounded firefly. You flap your wings but cannot rise. You still have light within that shines on and off yet in God there is no grounding. You will rise above any situation. Your light from within will stay bright and steady. The power from your faith can move mountains so never give up on any task that seems impossible

Chief BJ, 1997©

SPIRITUAL COMMENTARY ON FEAR

THIS IS A summary of a spiritual commentary that I received from meditation.

Fear is what keeps most of us on earth from accomplishing what needs to be done on our soul's journey. It is important for us to learn how to not stress out on things we cannot control. It is important for us not to let fears hamper us from accomplishing our life purposes.

Why do we have fears? We have fears or sometimes fear because we don't trust our spiritual high sense, or higher self. What is the spiritual high sense, or higher self? "This is the soul essence of our being." Just as there is a sensor in a car door opener to open the garage, or a sensor to activate computer programs, or a sensor on trucks and cars used to prevent the driver from hitting objects by alerting with a beeping sound, there is a similar sensor in our spiritual make-up.

Fear is not the conscious speaking. The conscious is the sensor for our moral and ethical make-up. The conscious immediately alerts us if we are doing something "wrong;" Something wrong against our moral and ethical principles, or something "wrong" against the universal laws.

Fear is a feeling of disconnection and unknowingness. The higher sensor operates within us, pretty much the way a battery functions in an automobile. We are body, mind and spirit. The physical and spiritual selves are carbon copies of each other. They are "twin selves" talking to each other. Sometimes these selves are in disagreement with each other. When the spiritual body and physical body selves are not in agreement, the mind does not receive a clear signal from the battery or sensor of the higher self. This may be likened to, a cell phone user's conversation, being unclear because he or she is out of range from a telephone satellite receiving station, or being totally disconnected, landing in a "dead zone" of silence.

Where does the fear come from? When the communication lines of connection are broken with the higher self, we are in an unknown zone (A place of unfamiliarity). We are in a place of discomfort. Our "spiritual higher self" has become disconnected and separated from God. "The physical body creates the fear." "The spiritual body or higher self knows no fear!"

December 2005
Jeanetta W. Dunlap, Ed.D.

Thoughts Matter

By thought we set into motion what happens. We are creators of our own destiny. Think only positive outcomes and bring about changes for the better. Be an optimist for, the pebbles of thought you toss into the water will cause a ripple effect. Negative thought brings negative return but the positive can reverse a negative situation and bring back the still waters.
Try it.

Chief BJ, 1997 ©

REFLECTION WORKSHEET
Making The Connection

Before reading the personal narrative vignette, identify any prior assumptions and beliefs that relate to this fear type.

THOUGHTS MATTER

THE CONCEPT OF fear is "thought-based." Thoughts are real, once created they develop or create a life form of their own.

Thoughts Matter.

What Is Thoughts Are Things?
Henry Van Dyke, American Contemporary Novelist and Poet

I hold it true that thoughts are things?
    They're endowed with bodies and breath and wings:
And that we send them forth to fill
    The world with good results, or ill
That which call our secret thought
    Speeds forth to earth's remotest spot,
Leaving its blessings or its woes
    Like tracks behind it as it goes.
We build our future, thought by thought,
    For good or ill, yet knows it not.
Yet so the universe was wrought.
    Thought is another name for fate;
Choose thy destiny and wait,

    For love brings love and hate brings hate.

I translate the verses of the poem to mean that thoughts are our inner feelings. Thoughts = Energy in motion. We can use our emotions to create thoughts for good or ill. Our emotions are outward expressions of our inner feelings. If that thought energy in motion is of good will then positive energy is set in motion. If the thought energy in motion is not of good will, and of the highest and best for God's Infinite Universe and all that inhabits the universe, then havoc reigns! This is why each of us needs to learn how to make our thoughts into spiritual things (Spiritual energy) so that only good will be created.

The universal law of attraction and the supporting creation formula, Thoughts = Energy in motion are in place from our births. There were times in my life that I blamed some of the obstacles in my life as being brought on by "unlucky" circumstances. I have now become aware that my thoughts create many of the situations in my life, pleasant and unpleasant. Therefore, I make a conscious effort daily to frame my thoughts (spoken and unspoken).

God said in Genesis, "Let there be light!" Our thoughts should create the light not the darkness. Sometimes dark is good. When we need a quiet place to rest, to be neutral while we reassess and energize, the darkness is not negative. Were we not in our Mother's womb before incarnating? I know this seems a strange concept, but everything in this Infinite Universe has a positive and negative side. Thus, there is dark and there is darkness versus light. Dark is a spiritual place of rest and darkness is not of the light!

God is a creator. Jesus is a creator and we are each creators. Did not God make us in His image? Did not Jesus say, "Whatever I do you can do greater things?" All that which is created is created with the WORD. The spoken WORD, how is it created? The word is created from thoughts and manifested into the physical.

During the years, I have suffered with the dis-ease of allergies. Finally, I began to find relief through homeopathic practices. One day looking in the mirror, I noticed that my eyes had cleared dramatically – no longer looking red and cloudy. A condition, I had resigned myself to. Looking in the mirror, I was very pleased with what I saw. While reflecting on this positive change, I had a fearful negative thought – "Suppose something or some accident happens to change this."

I didn't give this another thought, until at the end of the day, I noticed that one of my eyes was very, very red. I recalled that while arranging flowers, I had touched my eye with the floral powder used to extend the life of the flower cuttings. This accident required a visit to my optometrist. I was relieved to know, I had no eye damage. The moral of this situation – I should have accepted the blessings of the changes in my allergy condition and not have been fearful that the condition would return!

Worry can create fear. I CREATED WITH A FEARFUL THOUGHT, THE VERY CONDITION I DID NOT WANT TO MANIFEST.

AFFIRMATIONS

1. "I will avoid becoming bogged down by frustration and self-pity. This interferes with positive actions."

2. "I know that the WORD is created from thoughts and manifested into the physical. Jesus and I are co-creators. I can create, "In the name of Jesus . . ." (State manifestation goal)

POSITIVE THINKING MANIFESTATION ACTIVITIES

The unknown poet of this poem, does not say, "This is how to create spiritual thoughts," but I believe that if one lives by the tenets espoused, positive spiritual energy can be created.

Ten Thoughts To Live By
(Author Unknown)

1. Thou shalt not worry, for worry is the most unproductive of all human activities.

2. Thou shalt not be fearful, for most of the things we fear never come to pass.

3. Thou shalt not cross bridges before you get to them, for no one yet has succeeded in accomplishing this.

4. Thou shalt face each problem as it comes. You can handle only one at a time anyway.

5. Thou shalt not take problems to bed with you, for they make poor bedfellows.

6. Thou shalt not borrow other people's problems. They can take better care of them than you can.

7. Thou shalt not try to relive yesterday for good or ill-it is gone. Concentrate on what is happening in your life today.

8. Thou shalt count thy blessings, never overlooking the small ones, for a lot of small blessings add up to a big one.

9. Thou shalt be a good listener, for only when you listen do you hear ideas different from your own, it is very hard to learn something new when you are talking.

10. Thou shalt not become bogged down by frustration, for 90 percent of it is rooted in self-pity, and it will interfere with positive action.

BRAIN-BASED THOUGHT CHANGING ACTIVITY

In order, for a desire or a goal to be manifested, we have to impress a particular feeling upon our subconscious mind.

This is an activity that I have found to be helpful. I call it "Thought Watching."
Set a timer for 5 minutes, 10 minutes, or 15 minutes. When the timer rings, examine your thoughts.

Ask yourself, "Is it an empowering thought?" If, it seems to be a persistent negative thought, use *Thought Substitution* – Replace the negative thought with a positive thought.

REFLECTION WORKSHEET
Making The Connection

After reading the personal narrative vignette, reflect on these journaling prompts to answer questions that relate to this fear type. Are there shift changes in assumptions and beliefs? If so, why did they shift? If no shift, explain why.

1. What new beliefs are needed to confront my fear?

2. What "new" strategies do I need to develop in order to overcome my fear?

3. How willing am I to use strategic tools to overcome my fear?

4. What are the benefits of accepting the "new" changes in beliefs?

5. How can I develop a spiritual "Fear-Free" action plan and live it?

Making the connection . . . My Implementation Plan

Success-Itis Phobia

The Truth About... Fears, Blessings, and Disasters

A way will be shown, a door will open and you will escape the deterrents, blockages that hold you back from success. Just ask for God's guidance in the highest and best of ways. It may not be in the way you would like but a way will be shown for you to advance. In faith, you are led by hand, head, and heart. Even when you stray, you are guided back to God's flock just by asking.

Chief BJ, 1997 ©

REFLECTION WORKSHEET
Making The Connection

Before reading the personal narrative vignette, identify any prior assumptions and beliefs that relate to this fear type.

SUCCESS-ITIS PHOBIA

The Truth About . . . Fears, Blessings, and Disasters

THE BOOK OF Numbers in the Old Testament is named for the census of the Exodus generation taken at Mount Sinai (Numbers 1: 1-2) and for the census of the generation born in the wilderness taken on the plains of Moab (Numbers 26:2). The first generation of Israelites proved faithless, but the second generation made it to the promise land. Why did one group reap God's blessings and another did not?

If you or I are to reach the Promise Land and reap the blessings that God has in store, we must listen! If we do not listen, we are accepting and choosing that which is barren, that which does not bear fruit. With every decision there is usually a challenge. The challenge comes with a fork or crossroads in our lives. Often this is where we lose our blessings. We take the wrong road or we stay in neutral and let the environmental elements decide our travel itinerary for us, or we talk ourselves out of the blessings, or we may have fear.

Some of the thought energy, we put into motion in the universe may be these questions. Often we ask ourselves, "What is this going to cost me?" I want you to know that no matter what the cost, it is always best to be obedient to God. Remember the expression, "What goes around comes around?" God will keep bringing the same lessons into our lives in different ways hoping that, "We will get it!!!" We are living in an Earth School. If we successfully learn the lessons, God rewards us with blessings. The hymn, "There Shall Be Showers Of Blessings" affirms this, "There shall be showers of blessings ... This is the promise of love ... sent from the Savior," and is supported by Ezekiel 34: 26, "I will send down the showers in their season; they shall be showers of blessings."

If we are disobedient, we lose our blessings. This is not because God is a wrathful God who punishes us. This is because of our poor use of free will. If we choose not to follow spiritual laws, the blessings may never manifest, or we may obtain them and lose them. How can we lose our blessing inheritance as promised by Jesus? "Want to not obtain your blessings?" "Want to lose your blessings?" The recipe is within this essay. The main ingredient is fear!!!

I had an occasion to visit a relative for a celebratory event. I received the invitation in an untimely manner, no time to get a monthly air discount rate. Airplane transportation was required. I telephoned an airline carrier for reservation. The agent gave me a fantastic price for the trip! He asked for my charge card number. An unrealistic fear overcame me. I recalled news accounts about credit card theft. I thanked the airline agent and decided not to place the order by phone.

My intention was to buy the airline ticket from the airport. I parked at the local airport and went to the designated airline counter. I asked for a ticket to my designation, and was given a price that was one-hundred dollars more than the previous quote. I told the agent that I had called earlier and received a lower quote. The agent checked for the quote on the computer, but could not find it! He stated, that maybe, the quote had been a special discount, but now no longer available. I purchased my ticket at the counter. On the way home, I was angry at myself for having had "unreasonable fear." God had given me a blessing, but I lost it. I lost the blessing, because I chose not to practice the spiritual law of abundance. My earlier request to God for a discount ticket was manifested, but I used my free will foolishly, and lost my blessing. I not only paid more for the ticket, I had the extra cost for airport parking. Below is a recipe to follow, if you want to give back to God the blessings He wants to gift you.

Recipe For Losing Your Blessings

We lose blessings when we begin to fear. What is fear? "Fear is an assault on the mind." Fear is the cause of a troubled heart. Fear can keep you locked in a prison of isolation. Accurate biblical principled knowledge can help us face fears and put them to *sleep*.

We lose blessings when we violate spiritual law. We lose blessings when we choose to doubt Father-Mother God. We need to trust Father-Mother God when the way does not seem to be clear. If you or I do not choose faith, but rather choose to operate out of fear, we will suffer!!! Disasters will fall into our lives like rain drops.

The Israelites spies were looking through their eyes, not through the eyes of God. They saw themselves as helpless against their enemies. They focused on their lack of abilities. Thereby, forgetting that Father-Mother God is omnipotent, omnipresent, and omniscient. This lack of focus brought disaster into their lives.

Why are there obstacles? Father-Mother God allows us to walk in pain to make us like Him/Her. God is strengthening our faith, making us like His son Jesus the Christ I Am. God is refining us through obstacles and hindrances. Our individual decisions affect today (present) and tomorrow (future). Trust in Father-Mother God so that you don't have to ask, "What have I missed?" or, "What blessing did I miss?"

AFFIRMATIONS

1. "I listen to the God voice within me."

2. "I embrace success rather than fear."

3. "I embrace abundance."

REFLECTION WORKSHEET
Making The Connection

After reading the personal narrative vignette, reflect on these journaling prompts to answer questions that relate to this fear type. Are there shift changes in assumptions and beliefs? If so, why did they shift? If no shift, explain why.

1. What new beliefs are needed to confront my fear?

2. What "new" strategies do I need to develop in order to overcome my fear?

3. How willing am I to use strategic tools to overcome my fear?

4. What are the benefits of accepting the "new" changes in beliefs?

5. How can I develop a spiritual "Fear-Free" action plan and live it?

Making the connection . . . My Implementation Plan

Things Are Not Always What They Seem

Seeing is believing but in believing we can see. Too bad we have to have the facts proven to us before we believe. In most perplexities, proof must be given before we comprehend. Spiritual conveyance is assumed but inconsequential because of ignorance to one's power within. With trust and faith in God doors open to the Spirit within where one may find his own truth and wisdom for any need.

Chief BJ, 1997 ©

REFLECTION WORKSHEET
Making The Connection

Before reading the personal narrative vignette, identify any prior assumptions and beliefs that relate to this fear type.

THINGS ARE NOT ALWAYS WHAT THEY SEEM

THIS MORNING, I awakened to the sun (the son, Jesus) bathing my face in light. After a moment, I looked out of the window and watched the sun ascend between the branches of the evergreen trees. The sky was beautifully lit! The sky was a color canvas of pink, rose, green, and white, and hues of blues and purples. The same kinds of colors that you see when you use a wand to blow soap bubbles into the air. The colors I saw, I believe must be similar to the colors in the heavenly world. Many, who have had the opportunity to have near death experiences and then return to earth, state that the colors are of such a brilliancy that there are no words to describe.

As I watched the clouds and the sky, I was somewhat frightened, because an earlier weather watch announcement had scrolled on the bottom of the television screen. The weather announcement declared a secure weather watch for the surrounding counties until 11:00 P.M. I began to feel dread. I turned off the television and became quiet, and began to send out the "White Light" around my home and the homes of my neighbors and the neighborhood.

The severe thunder storm never arrived. Now in my after thoughts, I regret that I did not fully enjoy that moment. I let the fear of the moment and of the supposedly "to be" severe thunder storm hinder my clarity of the moment. The fear hindered my joy, the wonder of the event, and of being in the moment. Later, the eleven o'clock meteorologist's weather report, revealed that this event had a scientific name. This event does not happen very often, occurring every five years. I felt cheated. I allowed a weather forecast to make me fearful.

Have you ever allowed a person, or a situation to "get you going?" "To deprive you of something?" Did you later regret the behavior you exhibited in the situation? Often when we do things in the "heat of the moment" because we are angry or have fear, we later have lingering regrets about our actions or the way we allowed ourselves to behave or feel.

In my after thoughts, I am reminded of the scripture that, "God is light" (1 John 1:5). 1 John continues to say that, "God is light and in Him there is no darkness." God is *pure* light. Pure light radiates the chakra colors. What I saw on that Monday was the manifestation of God in pure light, in all of His glory!!! I was reminded that "Things Are Not Always What They Seem!!!"

There are light and dark forces. Ask yourself, "What would happen if there was no sunlight?" "Would plants grow?" The answer is, without sunlight, plant life will cease to grow. The plants will wither and die. When we don't feed, or tend to our personal spiritual garden, our spiritual self will wither and die. There are many people who pay for lawn services, or spend a lot of money fertilizing the lawn, and removing weeds, and watering the lawn to make sure it is green and luxurious looking. "What would happen if we spent as much time and care for our spiritual self?"

Why should we stay in the light?

If you stay in the light, you will find happiness and you will be able to maintain happiness. Wouldn't you rather be happy than unhappy? If we stay in the light we will find a way of living a harmonious life and peace of mind. Wouldn't you like to have peace of mind?

How do we stay in the light?

We can stay in the light, if we learn to create an atmosphere of light in our environment, whether it be home, work, or recreation. "Tend to your Spiritual garden." "Weed your Spiritual garden." "Weedwack your mind," "Weedwack your soul," and Weedwack your emotions."

Some individuals believe that the best way to make a prophecy about the future is the past. Each of us needs to know and understand what events have brought us to this time in our lives. God reveals Himself and His consciousness through our free will. If we begin to understand who we are, we will come to know our life purpose.

When we embark on learning the answers to these questions, we will learn how to tend to our spiritual garden. We will begin using our free will to make decisions that are more God-centered and not based on our anger or self-importance. Kermit the frog sang about being a frog in a human world. The song was entitled, "It Ain't Easy Being Green." In the song, Kermit talks about how difficult it is to be a frog because of his non-human looks. How many times have you struggled with "being you?"

I find that it is often hard trying to be me. Even if we think that we have an idea of who we are and set out on a path to be that "Me," we run into the challenges that Kermit the frog ran into. Kermit said, "I am a frog living in a human world." "Are not you and I, spiritual beings made in God's Light Image, living in a human/materialistic world?" We have the same challenges to overcome as Kermit.

Does not the sun light make its presence known? There are times we cannot ignore the presence of the sun (e.g., high summer heat temperature). There are times we cannot ignore the lack of the sun's presence. We may become cold, or depressed. Whatever, the circumstances, the presence of the sun light or the lack of sun light, is always noticed. Ask yourself, "Am I being noticed in the way I would like to be?" If the answer is no, maybe you are not "green" enough! There is an animal that is called a chameleon (It can change its colors to fit into the environment). Are you perhaps trying too hard to "blend in" to be like everybody else? Rev. Joyce Myers calls this "pleaser addiction." I go one step further by referring to this as a suffering from a disease. Dis-ease that is creating disharmony for the spiritual self-body, mind, and soul. If you and I don't learn to obtain harmony with the "I AM" in ourselves, we will live in constant conflict.

Conflict will not lead to harmony and peace of mind. Everything you and I expect from the future has its roots in our past. So the next time, you and I run into a Kermit the frog challenge in our human world, as a result of being ourselves, be it in the work place, the home, with a neighbor, or shopping, or wherever, maybe, we need to ask, "How do I fit into this situation?" We need to use our free will to "Fully Rely On God." Fully relying on God will create an atmosphere around us that will be connected to God's pure white light. This will permit us from being affected by others' anger, haste, or hurry. Nor, will we permit ourselves to be paralyzed by the Unknown!

AFFIRMATIONS

Don't allow yourself to be sorry about missed opportunities. If you have missed some opportunities, "Let go, "Let God." Move on. There are, and again, will be other opportunities for you. The opportunities are just delayed. God is Alpha and Omega. Alpha meaning He has no beginning and Omega meaning He has no end. Know therefore, there will always be opportunities. Opportunities are unlimited!

Become a frog groupie. There once was a Will Smith hip hop expression, "Let's get jiggy." "Let's get froggy-

(F) Fully

(R) Rely

(O) On

(G) God!"

Then you will always remain in the light.

AFFIRMATIONS

1. "I affirm that I will Let Go and Let God."

2. "I affirm that I will fully rely on God. I am in God's Light. Therefore, I am always in the moment without fear of the unknown."

POSITIVE THINKING MANIFESTATION ACTIVITIES

VISUALIZATION

Make an audio recording: The Bible tells us that Jacob gave his son Joseph a coat embroidered with beautiful colors. Picture a night sky with beautiful shining stars. A beautiful coat falls from the heaven into your hands. The coat is perfect. It has no imperfections. The starlight shines brilliantly on the coat highlighting the chakra colors. You are told by a voice from heaven, "This coat is the armour of God, spoken of in Ephesians (6:11)." "Put on the whole armour of God, that ye may be able to stand against the wiles of the devil." You adorn the coat. You know, and believe that, "God's coating" of the Father, Son, and Holy Spirit will shield you, from all the known and unknown imperfections in the world, including your own imperfections.

"Fully Rely On God" and let God's beautiful coat, made of the white light, become your daily armour of protection.

REFLECTION WORKSHEET
Making The Connection

After reading the personal narrative vignette, reflect on these journaling prompts to answer questions that relate to this fear type. Are there shift changes in assumptions and beliefs? If so, why did they shift? If no shift, explain why.

1. What new beliefs are needed to confront my fear?

2. What "new" strategies do I need to develop in order to overcome my fear?

3. How willing am I to use strategic tools to overcome my fear?

4. What are the benefits of accepting the "new" changes in beliefs?

5. How can I develop a spiritual "Fear-Free" action plan and live it?

Making the connection . . . My Implementation Plan

Suicide and Light Beyond Darkness

Release the negativity, let it go with each exhale of breath and bring in positive thought as you inhale. This is the cleansing of the inner body, mind, and soul. It allows God's light to heal while it flows freely through your being. Bring light to the darkness within so there will only be room for love. As you become more aware of this, you will have more respect for God and your body temple.

Chief BJ, 1997 ©

REFLECTION WORKSHEET
Making The Connection

Before reading the personal narrative vignette, identify any prior assumptions and beliefs that relate to this fear type.

SUICIDE AND LIGHT BEYOND DARKNESS

THIS IS A topic that is not one of my choosing. At the end of January 2005 and the beginning of February 2005, my meditation sessions began to impress suicide as an essay topic. I tried to change the topic, but found it impossible to write about another subject. With that said, my belief system tells me that God does not make errors or mistakes. Therefore, I write with confidence that God wanted me to write about this topic. Perhaps, someone needs to read this essay. Perhaps, someone reading, this essay will be able to identify with this topic (Either for themselves, a loved one, family member, or friend). The confirmation for this topic was made when I received a telephone call in the evening on a Tuesday, in January 2005.

The phone call, I received was from a friend who called to say that, she had gone to a church activity, and prayer was led for an elementary school-aged child in the church, who had attempted suicide. The child later died, and she was among those forming a grief team, to discuss the child's death with the other children in the church. She and I explored ideas as to how this subject might be discussed with the children and teenagers in the church. During that telephone conversation, I knew that this was God's confirmation for the subject that I had been hemming and haw-ing about, and not wanting to write.

I shared with the person on the other end of the line, experiences that I had encountered with children and teenagers in my work environment. My first experience, was when a bus driver made radio contact as he was driving to the school in the morning, to state that a boy, one of my students was trying to attempt suicide on the bus.

Another occasion several years later, found me face-to face with a group of boys and girls in my office. The teenagers were there to tell me that one of their classmates had been in the bathroom too long. They were concerned, because during lunch he had told them that he planned to kill himself!

There was another event. A female student's mother came to my office one morning to tell me that her daughter would not be in school that day. She had cut her wrists the night before and was in the hospital. She wanted to know how I and the school staff could help her with this situation.

Suicide is not immune to children and teenagers, or to ethnic groups, or to the religious practices they keep. Age also know no barriers! Those persons making a decision to end their existence on this earth plane may have an age number in the single digits, or decade numbers.

What may cause an individual to take his or her life? The suicide of any child, or teenager, or adult presents a unique set of circumstances for each individual and their families. Suicide is a reaction to overwhelming feelings of loneliness, worthlessness, helplessness, hopelessness, and depression. Some experts in the mental health professions believe suicide occurs when a person's pain exceeds his or her resources to cope with whatever is bothering them at that present moment and time. I would add to this list, fear. I would restate the sentence, "Suicide occurs when a person's fear of living exceeds his or her pain, and resources to cope with whatever is bothering them, at that moment in time to continue life."

Several February meditations provided this information:

Question: "Does Suicide solve problems?"

Answer: "No." "The person who takes his life will have to continue to deal with the problems after the transition death has been made."

Question: "What happens after suicide?"

Answer: "The spirit entity is held in the Hall of Learning."

"Healing takes place in the Hall of Learning, but before souls can go to the Hall of Learning, they must go to a Hall of Justice and assume responsibility for their actions. This is where the review of the life situation begins. This is different from the review we have, when we see our whole life review when we make the transition death naturally. Persons taking their own lives do not have a *whole life review* because they have left the earth plane too soon, before they were to leave. They find out that the problem was not solved, but is still with them. They review their life until the point of suicide, and they keep reviewing the act that took their life, until they can discover and pinpoint what made them so desolate, so depressed, so hopeless, that they thought this was the only way out, the only way they could solve their problem."

During this same week, the Holy Spirit, the Comforter led me to this internet poem.
Web Address: lightoflove.net
Direct link for this card verse: Lightoflove.net/Special/GodLovesYou.htm

It is my belief that this poem can comfort those who have had loved ones make the death transition by suicide.

I said,
God, I hurt."
And God said,
"I know."

I said,
"God, I cry a lot."
And God said,
"That is why I gave you tears."
I said,
"God, I am so depressed."
And God said,
"That is why I gave you sunshine."

I said,
"God, life is so hard."
And God said,
That is why I gave you loved ones."

I said,
"God, my loved one died."
And God said,
"So did mine.

I said,
"God it is such a loss."
And God said,
"I saw mine nailed to a cross."

I said,
"God where are they now?"
And God said,
"Mine is on my right and yours is
in the Light."

AFFIRMATIONS

1. "Only God creates life. I value my life and the life of others. I find comfort in God's divine unjudgmental love."

2. I affirm, "We are all God's children." "No one has the right to judge the other." "We are all God's children."

3. I affirm, "Each time I mistreat myself or others, I am harming our soul's development, and contributing to disharmony in the universe."

PRAYER

1. It is extremely important for us to remember those who have committed suicide in our daily prayers.

Write a personal prayer.

2. It is extremely important for us to pray daily for those known to us and unknown to us who may be thinking of suicide.

Write a personal prayer.

VISUALIZATION

1. Read these phrases: Be Mine, 2) Forever Yours, and 3) I Love You.

Close your eyes and think of God. Think of God as related to these expressions. Meditate on each of this phrases one at a time – Be Mine, Forever Yours, and I Love You.

Now end your meditation with pictures of your loving relationship with God. Know that God wants us to be Forever His, to Love Him, and to know He loves us eternally.

2. Read these phrases: 1) Be Mine, 2) Forever Yours, and 3) I Love You.
   Read the phrases silently and then aloud.
   Identify the phrase that resonates *the* most with you. Write the phrase. Meditate on the phrase. Contemplate on your loving relationship with God.

REFLECTION WORKSHEET
Making The Connection

After reading the personal narrative vignette, reflect on these journaling prompts to answer questions that relate to this fear type. Are there shift changes in assumptions and beliefs? If so, why did they shift? If no shift, explain why.

1. What new beliefs are needed to confront my fear?

2. What "new" strategies do I need to develop in order to overcome my fear?

3. How willing am I to use strategic tools to overcome my fear?

4. What are the benefits of accepting the "new" changes in beliefs?

5. How can I develop a spiritual "Fear-Free" action plan and live it?

Making the connection . . . My Implementation Plan

Entertaining Angels Unaware

Precepts, concepts, the head spins in the universal flow. It is difficult to sort out our needs. We try to digest the inner yield even when mixed emotions spill out. Do we listen to angels or to fools? Are we subdued in spiritual conquests? Always ask that the Christ light of protection be put around you and that you always receive truth and wisdom in the highest and best of ways.

Chief BJ, 1997 ©

REFLECTION WORKSHEET
Making The Connection

Before reading the personal narrative vignette, identify any prior assumptions and beliefs that relate to this fear type.

ENTERTAINING ANGELS UNAWARE

"Do not neglect to show hospitality to strangers, for by doing that some have entertained angels without knowing it." (Hebrews 13:2)

THE PATRIARCH ABRAHAM and his wife Sarah had an opportunity to entertain angels unaware. Abraham and Sarah reach out in hospitality to three strangers offering them a meal. They later find that they are heavenly strangers.

One very early snowy wintry morning. I was shoveling the snow out of the driveway. I had just about completed the job, when I looked up and a middled aged woman was standing in front of me. She explained to me that her car had broken down, and she needed to make a phone call. This was in the days before portable phones or cell phones.

Without thinking, I invited the woman into my home to use the telephone. She made her phone call, and said that her son would be picking her up. I was becoming somewhat agitated, because I needed to get dressed for work, and also by now I am having second thoughts about having invited a stranger into my home. I began to think fearfully. I had thoughts about my safety. It was as though the woman could read my thoughts. She said she would leave now.

She left, and I proceeded to see where she would go. I am feeling guilty about my feelings of fear, and sending the woman out into the wintry cold. As I looked out of the window, a car drove up and parked in front of the house across the street. She got into the car, and the car disappeared in mid air!!!!!!!!!!!!!

I stood in front of the window in shock. Then I remembered the Biblical scripture of Hebrews 13:2. I then began to recall statements that didn't quite make sense. The woman told me that her son would pick her up from my house. How did he get there? I didn't hear her give an address. When she approached me, she said her car had broken down. I don't recall seeing a car near my house or my neighbors' houses.

Indeed if the car had broken down somewhere else, why would she walk so far to find my home by passing the commercial center of stores before my home is reached? I don't have the answers, but I know without a doubt that I saw the car dematerialize in mid air. I do believe the woman was an angel. Why did she come to me? I don't have the answers. Maybe, it is as simple as the Biblical scripture, "Did God test me to see if I would show hospitality to a stranger in need?"

Discernment is needed when we encounter people we don't know. Who are the strangers? Anyone we do not know is a stranger – "Everyday people." Every stranger is a potential encounter with God. The stranger may be a messenger of God or your Guardian Angel. Some of the strangers we encounter are those with special needs. Some are in hospitals. Some are in prison. Some are deaf. Some are in places of worship. Some strangers are confused and afraid. Do you care enough to show hospitality to strangers? Learn to use discernment that is a gift from the Holy Spirit.

Know that when the gift of hospitality is offered, we are practicing the Golden Rule, "Whatsoever ye would that others should do unto you, do ye also unto them." Know that when the gift of hospitality is offered, we are practicing the Law of Attraction, "Whatever we put out into the universe is returned." Every stranger is a potential encounter with God. We may be entertaining God's messengers and not even know it!!!

AFFIRMATIONS

1. "I realize, by knowingly neglecting to show hospitality to strangers in need, I may be entertaining angels unaware."

2. "I ask for discernment when encountering strangers and care enough to show hospitality. I care enough to see "the Christ" in them. I know that whatever, I put into the universe is returned."

REFLECTION WORKSHEET
Making The Connection

After reading the personal narrative vignette, reflect on these journaling prompts to answer questions that relate to this fear type. Are there shift changes in assumptions and beliefs? If so, why did they shift? If no shift, explain why.

1. What new beliefs are needed to confront my fear?

2. What "new" strategies do I need to develop in order to overcome my fear?

3. How willing am I to use strategic tools to overcome my fear?

4. What are the benefits of accepting the "new" changes in beliefs?

5. How can I develop a spiritual "Fear-Free" action plan and live it?

Making the connection . . . My Implementation Plan

God's Decision Making

When going inward, one merges with the soul to find a mighty force. It brings peace, joy, love, truth, and wisdom because you are one with God in an inner chamber of all-knowing Divine Force. It is there for you to enjoy. Your very own temple of God, where you can find all your answers and an understanding that nothing is in vain, enlightenment comes to explain the cause. So use and respect your body temple.

Chief BJ, 1997 (c)

REFLECTION WORKSHEET
Making The Connection

Before reading the personal narrative vignette, identify any prior assumptions and beliefs that relate to this fear type.

GOD'S DECISION MAKING

IF YOU DO not like the direction your life is taking, your present decision making habits may be stopping you from getting your directions from God. How do you and I change the habits we have had a life time, to new habits?

This "new" habit is learning how to acquire spiritual discernment. Spiritual discernment means getting in the habit of acknowledging God and getting our directions from Him instead of acknowledging what seems to be right to us.

Saul the first King of Israel, was led down a road of defeat by doing what he thought was right. He kept to his own understanding and his habit led to his failure and defeat. In contrast, David acknowledged God and asked for His direction in his life. David faced Goliath, the giant with regular clothing, a sling shot, and some rocks. Without all the armor and the shields that Goliath had, David slew Goliath and freed the Israelites. David's habit of letting God direct his life, brought him to the throne of Israel as King David.

Before making a decision ask for guidance from the Holy Spirit in making your decision. The Holy Spirit will provide your answer with wisdom and discernment.

ASK.
Listen to the Holy Spirit.

If you hear a clear Yes, then the answer is YES.

If you hear a clear No, then the answer is NO.

If you don't hear a clear YES or NO, it is possible that God does not want any action taken at this time.

If you find that your decision was not of highest and the best – "A God decision," God permits U-Turns

> "Trust in the Lord with all your heart, and lean not on your own understanding. In all your ways acknowledge Him, and He [God] shall direct paths." (Proverbs 3:5-6)

AFFIRMATION

"I will acquire and use spiritual discernment in my decision making."

REFLECTION WORKSHEET
Making The Connection

After reading the personal narrative vignette, reflect on these journaling prompts to answer questions that relate to this fear type. Are there shift changes in assumptions and beliefs? If so, why did they shift? If no shift, explain why.

1. What new beliefs are needed to confront my fear?

2. What "new" strategies do I need to develop in order to overcome my fear?

3. How willing am I to use strategic tools to overcome my fear?

4. What are the benefits of accepting the "new" changes in beliefs?

5. How can I develop a spiritual "Fear-Free" action plan and live it?

Making the connection . . . My Implementation Plan

Change

Be encouraged with change,
for in change one grows. We
have to let go of the old and
welcome the new. Some habits
and people are hard to part with,
but if we want to grow for betterment
we must move
toward God's light. The memories
of good will always be there to
remind you of your growth. All
lessons learned are good. Our
world advances with invention
and discovery, so must we. Allow
spirit to lead you in light and love.

Chief BJ, 1997 ©

REFLECTION WORKSHEET
Making The Connection

Before reading the personal narrative vignette, identify any prior assumptions and beliefs that relate to this fear type.

CHANGE

NEW WORDS ARE coined in our society. Many of us are familiar with the newly coined words Pre-Approved and Pre-Qualified. Many advertisements come to millions of homes by postal mail declaring that the residents have already met the qualifications for Pre-Approved credit cards, are Pre-Approved for home mortgages, and personal loans. We are Pre-Qualified by God as divine beings. As divine beings we are entitled to live a fear-free life.

It is important to understand that in our Christian spiritual lives that change begins with endings! A fear-free life cannot begin until there is an ending process. Endings initiate waiting time. Waiting time must occur before the new beginnings can happen. Change is situational and really painless. It is the transition process for change that is painful; Our minds try to come to terms with the new situation. Change is what happens on the outside. Transition is what is happening on the inside. We can envision transition as being a type of waiting room (e.g., a hospital room). Visiting the hospital waiting room while someone is in surgery, can be a very unsettling, uncomfortable experience.

I am learning that God often uses "waiting time, or "waiting rooms" as cool downs to prepare us for the new encounters of life, or to prepare the way for our blessings to take place. We may ask, "When?" I have often asked God, "How long do I need to wait?" On the pre-approved and pre-qualified applications, we are warned of an offer deadline time or given an expiration date." Why is God's time not specific? We are human beings, mortals, and our "right now" attitudes, and our quick decisions sometimes wreck havoc with God's plans for us. We will be persecuted at times, "Yea all that will live godly in Christ Jesus will suffer persecution, "but tribulations will not overcome us"; Therefore being justified by faith, we have peace with God through our Lord Jesus Christ (2 Timothy 3:12).

While we are waiting, we need to realize that God doesn't often do things the way we expect. God doesn't perform His work sequentially like a novel. A novel starts with the beginning, has a middle, and then ends (happily or unhappily), or in some instances has no ending. Toni Morrison (Novelist of *Tar Baby, Sulah, Bluest Eye, and Beloved*; probably her most well known novel), is a writer who does not give definitive closure or endings to her novels. I had the opportunity to attend one of her lectures. When asked, why she did not give closure in her novels, she stated, "That's the way life is." "Life does not have closure."

What action can be taken while waiting for changes?

We have faith.
We have faith that we are pre-approved, pre-qualified for our blessing. This means that we affirm . . .

Faith is belief without seeing.
Faith is thanking God before we receive whatever we have asked for.
We have confidence in our ability to accept the positive change energy that will be manifested.
We affirm with faith, that we are Pre-Approved, Pre-Qualified for our blessing.

AFFIRMATION

"I will strengthen my faith and keep the forces of hope alive.
I know that God's waiting room door will open and I will walk out to new beginnings."

PRAYER
Prayers can be an intercession, a petition, or for thanksgiving. We may need to use each of these prayer types when we are in a change situation. The prayer below encompasses each of these features.

Pray . . .

Father-Mother God I ask for help during this uncomfortable time of change. Help me and others to use this waiting room time to learn from you, to praise you, and to give prayers of thanksgiving for the blessings we have not yet received, but know without a doubt that only the blessings of "the highest and best" will be given to us in your time, and given with your Grace and Mercy.

REFLECTION WORKSHEET
Making The Connection

After reading the personal narrative vignette, reflect on these journaling prompts to answer questions that relate to this fear type. Are there shift changes in assumptions and beliefs? If so, why did they shift? If no shift, explain why.

1. What new beliefs are needed to confront my fear?

2. What "new" strategies do I need to develop in order to overcome my fear?

3. How willing am I to use strategic tools to overcome my fear?

4. What are the benefits of accepting the "new" changes in beliefs?

5. How can I develop a spiritual "Fear-Free" action plan and live it?

Making the connection . . . My Implementation Plan

STAND ... STAND ... STAND

Combine the beautiful experiences in life with those that were painful. They were all needed for soul growth toward betterment. To receive enlightenment one must also face darkness. Acceptance of all experiences and keeping faith in God one will eventually find the green pasture and still water. We all have crosses to bear as Jesus did but must ask and pray for God's will to be our will.

Chief BJ, 1997 ©

REFLECTION WORKSHEET
Making The Connection

Before reading the personal narrative vignette, identify any prior assumptions and beliefs that relate to this fear type.

STAND . . . STAND . . . STAND . . .

I HAD BEEN wrestling with a troubling situation for almost three years. The second year everything came to "a head" to use that expression. Looking back over the years, I see that there were several things that I might have done to turn the tide of things. I should have made changes in the way I interacted with certain personalities. However, I excessively tried to be a "peacemaker." In the beatitudes, Jesus said, "Blessed are the peacemakers for they shall be called the children of God" (Matthew 5:9). In the divine sense, peacemakers are those who have a peaceable disposition. This position is to love, and desire to delight in peace. Persons who seek peace are blessed, because they are working together with Christ to proclaim peace on earth. There is a time to see the Christ in others, and then there is a time to take a stand against those who do not desire peace and those who do not desire the Christian experience.

The situation finally forced me to make changes. I needed to take a stand. I did not know what to stand about or how to stand. I was in a confused state of mind. My Great Grandmother wanted me to be like the tree in the psalm and in the song: "Like a tree planted by the water, I shall not be moved"! I understood the words, but I was still wavering and vacillating about a decision I had to make. I was truly not wanting to make "waves," and I had a fear of the unknown. I asked God for a sign, and that sign came to me in two ways. One of the signs was given to me on one of my morning walking treks. As I walked, each step seemed to be a cadence, **"stand"**, **"stand"**,

"**stand**" . . . While doing online research for a doctoral class that I was taking, I clicked on one of the subject links; A pop-up advertisement came on the computer monitor. When I attempted to close the pop-up screen, miraculously a two-part sermon by Rev. Bob Mumford entitled, "Standing in the Whirlwind" appeared. Exactly what I needed for my Spiritual Food. This was my second sign from God. I had asked God to give me a sign as to *what it meant to stand*, and once I knew what it meant to stand, *how to stand*. I also, asked God to give me the answers from a source, I would not expect. The Internet was the unexpected source.

Why do we have these situations? Rev. Mumford says, "Occasionally, I put it this way." "God fixes a fix to fix you. If you fix the fix before you are fixed, God has another fix to fix you." I interpreted this as God has lessons for us to learn and if we try to take care of "the something" on our own, or take action before "God's time," we will find ourselves in a category 5 weather advisory. Rev, Mumford's sermon taught me that, "If I learn not to be directed by circumstances, but by the will of God, then I have truly learned what it means to stand."

I have learned that, after I have done all I know how to do-prayed, praised, read the Bible, prophesied, and having been prophesied to, read all kinds of Spiritual literature, and asked others to pray for me, that sometimes that it is not enough! There comes a time that nobody can help me, but me. I had to learn to stand all by myself! The question I asked God was, "How do I stop the downward spiral of the whirlwind when my enemies are attacking me like a flood-attacking my mind, and my emotions, how do I stand???"

When the levies broke and the floodgates opened, I had to start remembering. I had to remember that, God has heard my prayers before and will this time also. I had to learn this time that there are times God will not intercede for us. He wants us to stand, so that we will ask His son Jesus the Christ to help us. I could not see what lay ahead. I could not see through the fog, I had to step out on faith; The faith of the mustard seed, to trust that Jesus would guide me and make my way clear. While I was traveling through the fog, I hurt mentally, physically, and spiritually. After, I trusted faithfully in Jesus, there were times that I could not stand. There were times I fell and faltered. This is when the Holy Spirit came to comfort me! By conquering successfully the whirlwind in my life, I learned and understood for the first time in my life the role of the Trinity (Father-Mother God, the Giver of divine love, Jesus Christ, the Master Healer, and the Holy Spirit, the Comforter).

As we come closer to the throne of Father-Mother God, and walk the road of obedience, the whirlwinds of Satan and his workers will blow harder, and sometimes become a tornado, or a hurricane category 5 proportion. When that tornado sweeps us in a whirlwind or the hurricane winds are destroying the safe places around us, it is imperative for us to stand in the whirlwinds. The formula is, "To stand on the promises of God the Father and Mother, the Son Jesus the Christ, and the Holy Spirit." "Let GO AND LET GOD" is the formula.

AFFIRMATIONS

1. "When the category five whirlwinds are destroying the safe places around me and others, I will STAND with God!"

2. "I will STAND on the the promises of the Trinity in the whirlwinds. I will let go and let God."

REFLECTION WORKSHEET
Making The Connection

After reading the personal narrative vignette, reflect on these journaling prompts to answer questions that relate to this fear type. Are there shift changes in assumptions and beliefs? If so, why did they shift? If no shift, explain why.

1. What new beliefs are needed to confront my fear?

2. What "new" strategies do I need to develop in order to overcome my fear?

3. How willing am I to use strategic tools to overcome my fear?

4. What are the benefits of accepting the "new" changes in beliefs?

5. How can I develop a spiritual "Fear-Free" action plan and live it?

Making the connection . . . My Implementation Plan

CONCLUSION

Contemplative Native American Legend

A YOUNG INDIAN brave went to the mountain to prove his manhood. He was very proud of himself, because he had accomplished his mountain climb. On the way down the mountain, a snake spoke to him, and said "Please help me. I am about to die. Please put me in your shirt and take me down the valley, so that I don't die of cold." The boy said, "You are a poisonous snake, you will kill me." "No said the snake. I will treat you differently. If you help me out, I will never harm you."

The boy kept resisting, and finally changed his mind, because the snake was very persuasive. He picked up the snake and carried the snake down the valley and laid it gently down. The snake coiled and bit the boy. The boy cried, "You made me a promise!" The snake said to him, "You knew what I was when you picked me up."

Lesson: "There are some things in life we better not pick up."

"FEAR is one of those things!"
Author's editorial addition.

GLOSSARY

1. God – Divine Mind and Spirit
   Infinite Creator of the Universe

2. Chakras – Seven energy channels of specific colors involving different parts of the body. (Jeanetta W. Dunlap, Ed.D.)

3. Fear – Learned and reinforced negative behavior.
   A discomforted feeling of disconnection and unknowingness.
   (Jeanetta W. Dunlap, Ed.D.)

4. Holy Spirit – Trinity of Three Persons: The Father (God), The Son (Jesus) and Holy Spirit (Comforter).
   R. A. Torrey (1996). *The Person and Working of the Holy Spirit.*

5. Jesus – Son of God, spiritual nucleus within each of us.

6. Light – Whiteness and purity
   The Christ Light – "I am the light of the world," (John 9:4-5)

7. Meditation-Contemplative technique of "resting in the silence" for spiritual growth.
   Jack Kornfield (2004). *Meditation For Beginners.*

8. Soul – That which is both conscious and subconscious developed out of spirit, carrying out the ideals of God.

9. Thought – Process in the mind in which substance is acted on by energy – movement of ideas into the mind.

Note: Unless otherwise indicated, definitions are from the *Metaphysical Bible Dictionary* (1995).

RECOMMENDED RESOURCES

Chief BJ's (Betty Smith) Inspirational Cards (1997)
A set of meditation cards designed to cultivate positive states of inner peace. Each card is a guided meditation for daily reflection.
Lily Dale Bookstore
c/o 5 Melrose Park
P.O. Box 248
Lily Dale, New York 14752-0248

Meditation For Beginners. Jack Kornfield (2004).
Distills the essential teachings and guided practices for learning transformative practices of meditation.
Sounds True, Inc. Boulder CO 80360

Metaphysical Bible Dictionary (1995)
Reference volume presenting esoteric meaning of key names, places, and vocabulary found in the Bible referenced on teachings of Jesus Christ.
Charles Fillmore Reference Library
Unity Books
Unity Village, MO 64065

Your Word is Your Wand: A Sequel to The Game of Life. Florence Scovel Shinn (1928).
A person's word is a wand with the power to change unhappy conditions.
DeVorss & Company Publisher
P.O. Box 550
Marina del Rey, CA 90294
Place order at local book stores.
Reprinted on-line as eBook in PDF form.
Available from Amazon.com

To contact the author

If you wish to contact the author please email: *spiritual.quest@gmail.com*

The writer cannot guarantee an answer to every correspondence, but the author will appreciate hearing from you, and learning how this book has helped you.

Additional books, can be ordered by contacting Xlibris Corporation. For information, please phone 1-888-795-4274 or email orders to orders@xlibris.com.